Ready or not, here we go!

A tiny sound echoes through the morning mist.

It is coming from an egg the size of a bowling ball hidden in the forest underbrush.

What's beneath the shell?
The egg shifts and shakes, until...

CRACKKK!

Diplodocus! He blinks as the bright sunlight spills
across the forest floor. He stretches his body from his
little head, to his trunk-like legs, to his whip-like tail.

Suddenly...

CRACKKK!

Another egg hatches.

CRACKKK!

And another.

But where's Mum? The Diplodocus hatchlings
stand up, ready to take on the world, until...

Smelling the damp air, **Allosaurus** slows. Allosaurus has two powerful legs, a massive body, razor-sharp teeth, and an enormous...

ROARRR!

The Diplodocus hatchlings **SCATTER!** Allosaurus smells the makings of a tasty morning snack.

SNIFF!

SNIFF!

SNIFF!

...little Diplodocus hides deep in the giant fern leaves to blend in. **Shrewd.**

Allosaurus comes closer and closer, but...

BOOM! BOOM!

Lucky for little Diplodocus, Allosaurus has found another dinosaur to chase.
Stegosaurus.

Phew!

Where did the other hatchlings go?

Diplodocus stops
to listen, but all
he hears is...

Rumble.

Grumble.

Grumble.

Is it another dinosaur? No! It's his belly!
He is a hungry herbivore, and his hiding
place is full of tasty leaves.

MUNCH. CHOMP. GULP.

He snacks on juicy ferns, waxy gingkoes, crunchy cycads – even some pebbles!

YUM!

MUNCH. CHOMP. GULP.

Diplodocus is growing **fast**,
so he needs to eat **a lot!**

With a full belly, Diplodocus dozes off
under a giant fern. But his slumber
doesn't last long because...

...someone is tickling his nose!

Flit. Flit. Flutter.

Flit. Flit. Flutter.

Libellulium has landed right on his nose.

Achoo!

Flit. Flit. Flutter.

Libellulium flutters away. **Spirited**.

Diplodocus bounds after it. *Wait!*

Maybe Libellulium knows
where Diplodocus's family is?

Libellulium flies on.

Diplodocus bounds along.

Weaving under the giant bellies of one, two, three **Brachiosauruses**.

Oh my!

Libellulium tiptoes across the spiky tail of a grazing Stegosaurus, and Diplodocus follows.

Shhhh!

Little Diplodocus zig-zags through the fleet feet of **Dryosaurus**.

And he runs away from the giant mouth and horned nose of **Ceratosaurus**.

As Libellulium flies off across the river, little Diplodocus's first adventure-filled day draws to a close, and all he can think of is...

FOOD!

Munch. Chomp. Gulp.

One day, Diplodocus will **GROW** into one of the longest and largest dinosaurs to ever walk the Earth.

But for now, he just wants to be with what he has been searching for all day.

Family!

Who was Diplodocus?

Diplodocus was a herbivore, which meant it ate plants for food.

Diplodocus was a huge dinosaur with a long neck and tail.

Diplodocus had little spines running along its back.

Diplodocus was one of the largest animals ever. A fully grown diplodocus was about as long as a blue whale!

Diplodocus travelled in big groups, called herds, for safety.

Diplodocus lived about 150 million years ago in what is now North America.

Diplodocus could use its tail like a whip to defend itself.

How to say...

Diplodocus
dip-LOD-oh-kus

Allosaurus
AL-oh-SORE-us

Stegosaurus
STEG-oh-SORE-us

Libellulium
li-BELL-ooh-lee-um

Brachiosaurus
brackee-oh-SORE-us

Dryosaurus
DRY-oh-SORE-us

Ceratosaurus
seh-RAT-oh-SORE-us

What do those words mean?

Carnivore
An animal that hunts and eats other animals.

Cycad
A type of plant common when dinosaurs lived.

Fern
A leafy plant that was eaten by lots of dinosaurs.

Ginkgo
One of the oldest types of trees.

Hatchling
A newly-hatched baby animal.

Herbivore
An animal that eats plants for food.

Jurassic
The second of the three time periods when dinosaurs lived.

Sauropod
A group of huge plant-eating dinosaurs.

About the illustrator

Marie Bollmann is a freelance illustrator who specialises in children's books. Marie was born in Münster, Germany, and is now based in Hamburg. She likes creating colourful, detailed illustrations, and her favourite dinosaur is Triceratops.

About the author

Elizabeth Gilbert Bedia is a former teacher and audiologist. She loves creating stories about our amazing world. She is the author of *Bess the Barn Stands Strong*, and *Balloons for Papa*. She lives in central Iowa with her dinosaur-loving family. You can visit her at www.elizabethgilbertbedia.com.

About the consultant

Dougal Dixon is a Scottish palaeontologist, geologist, author, and educator. He has written more than 100 books, including the seminal work of speculative biology *After Man*, and award-winning *Where the Whales Walked*.

Illustrator Marie Bollmann
Text for DK by Elizabeth Gilbert Bedia & Et Al Creative
Acquisitions Editors Fay Evans, James Mitchem
Project Art Editor Charlotte Bull
Consultant Dougal Dixon
Publishing Coordinator Issy Walsh
Senior Production Editor Nikoleta Parasaki
Senior Production Controller Inderjit Bhullar
Deputy Art Director Mabel Chan
Publishing Director Sarah Larter

First published in Great Britain in 2022 by
Dorling Kindersley Limited
DK, One Embassy Gardens, 8 Viaduct Gardens,
London, SW11 7BW

The authorised representative in the EEA is
Dorling Kindersley Verlag GmbH. Arnulfstr. 124,
80636 Munich, Germany

Illustrations copyright © Marie Bollmann 2022
Copyright in the layouts and design of
the work will vest in the publisher.
© 2022 Dorling Kindersley Limited
A Penguin Random House Company
10 9 8 7 6 5 4 3 2 1
001–327011–Sep/2022

A CIP catalogue record for this book
is available from the British Library.
ISBN: 978-0-2415-3849-4

Printed and bound in China

For the curious
www.dk.com

FSC
www.fsc.org
MIX
Paper | Supporting
responsible forestry
FSC™ C018179

This book was made with Forest Stewardship Council™ certified paper – one small step in DK's commitment to a sustainable future. For more information go to www.dk.com/our-green-pledge